PIANO SOLO

KEEP CALM
AND
PLAY ON

MW00799623

WISE PUBLICATIONS
part of The Music Sales Group

London / New York / Paris / Sydney / Copenhagen / Berlin / Madrid / Hong Kong / Tokyo

DISCOVERY AT NIGHT

Music by Ludovico Einaudi.

DOWNTON ABBEY

(THEME)

Music by John Lunn.

8

Poco meno mosso ♩ = 154

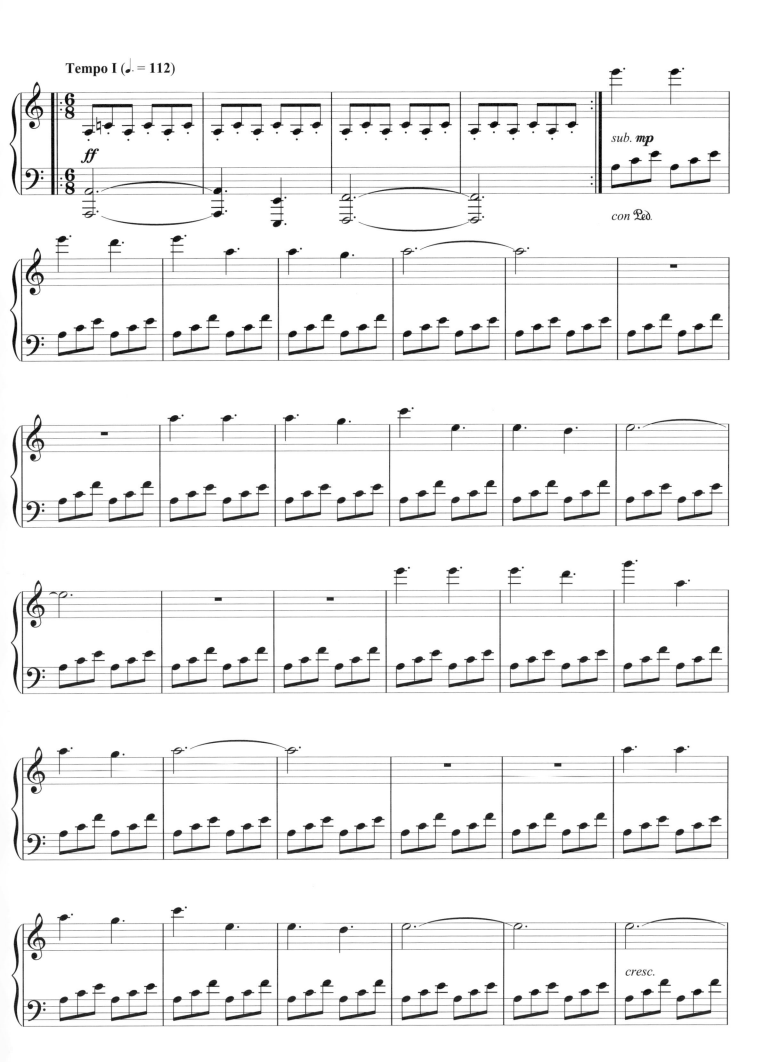

GAME OF THRONES

(MAIN TITLE)

Music by Ramin Djawadi.

19

A GOOD MORNING MELODY

Music by Zbigniew Preisner.

I cannot sleep, so I go outside, and see an unearthly view:
below my house window, everything is floating in fog, just as if the
mansion was hanging somewhere in clouds and flying.
It's a pity it doesn't fly.
How good that I couldn't sleep.

22

23

IT'S YOUR DAY

Music by Yiruma.

27

LA VALSE D'AMÉLIE

(FROM AMÉLIE)

Music by Yann Tiersen.

LONG, LONG TIME AGO/THE FUNERAL

(FROM PAN'S LABYRINTH)

Music by Javier Navarrete.

LONG, LONG TIME AGO

Moderato, rubato

Più mosso ♩ = 88

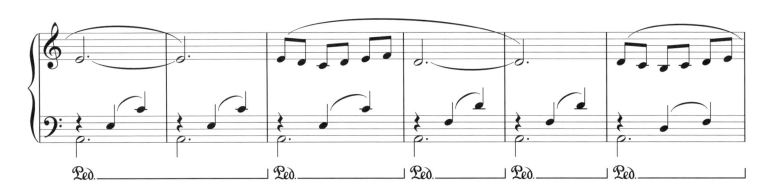

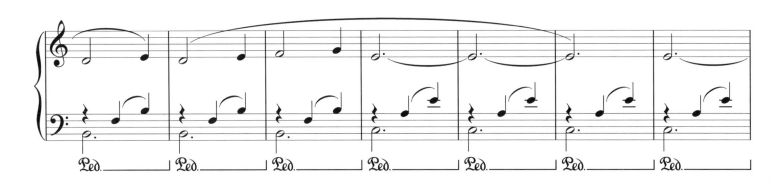

THE FUNERAL

L'IMAGINAIRE

(FROM SAUVE QUI PEUT LA VIE)

Music by Gabriel Yared.

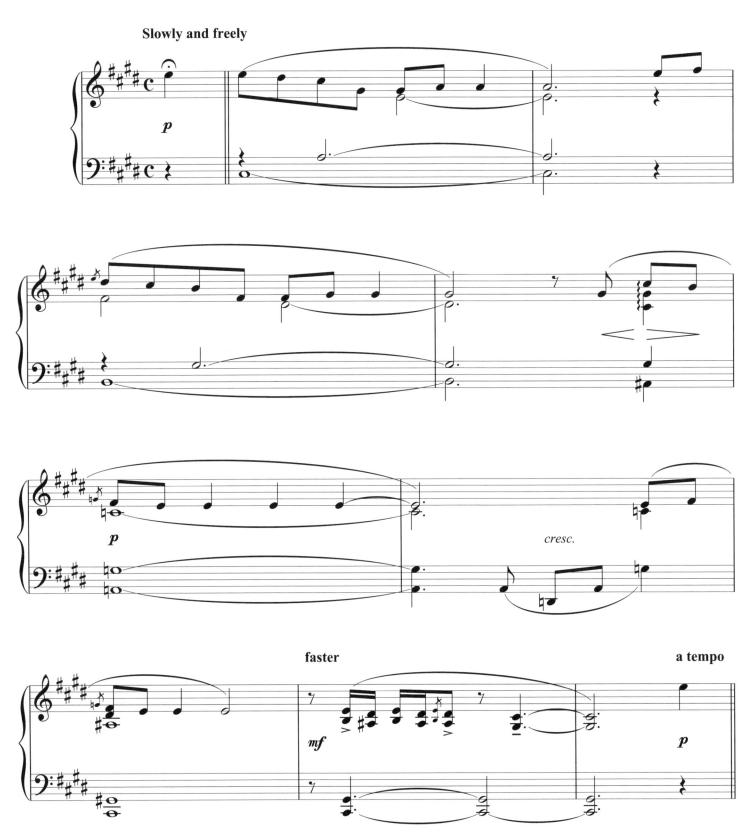

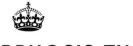

METAMORPHOSIS TWO

Composed by Philip Glass.

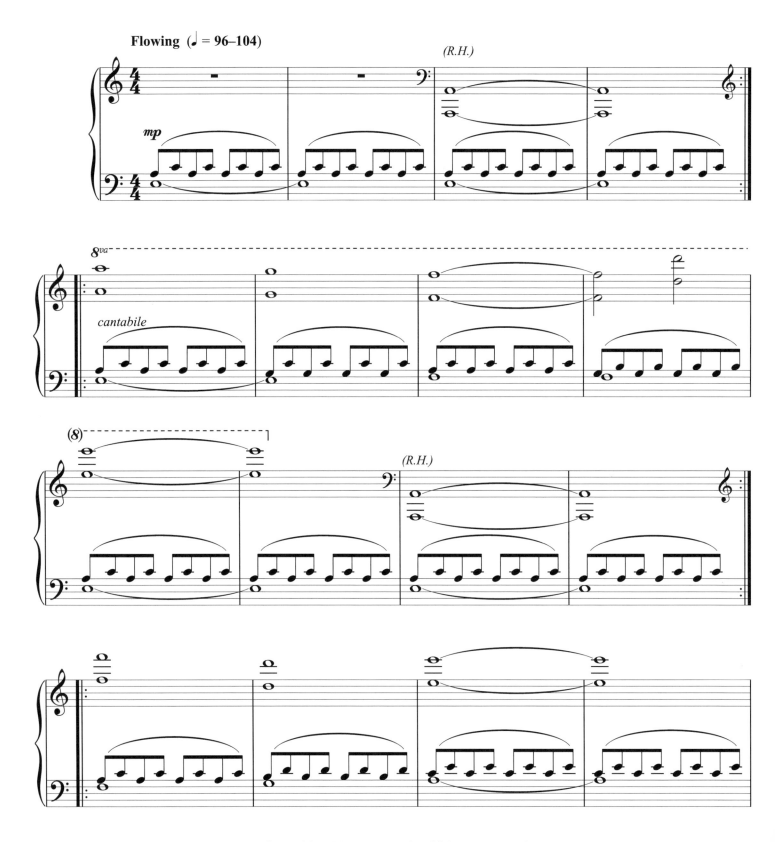

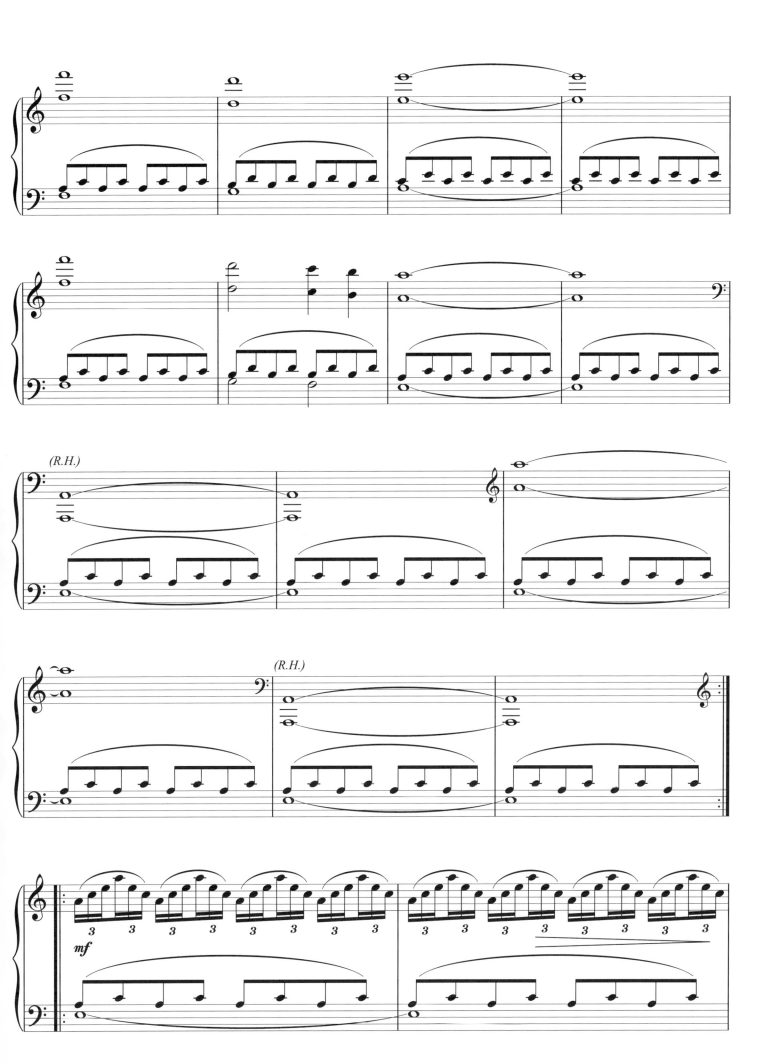

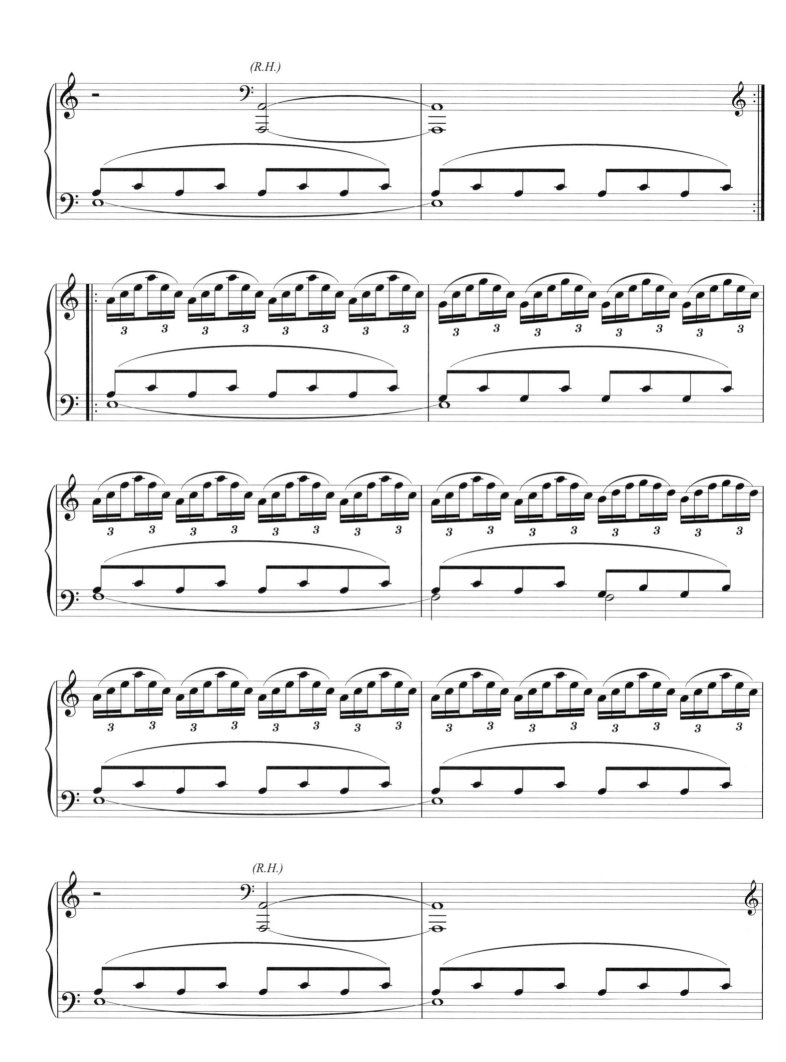

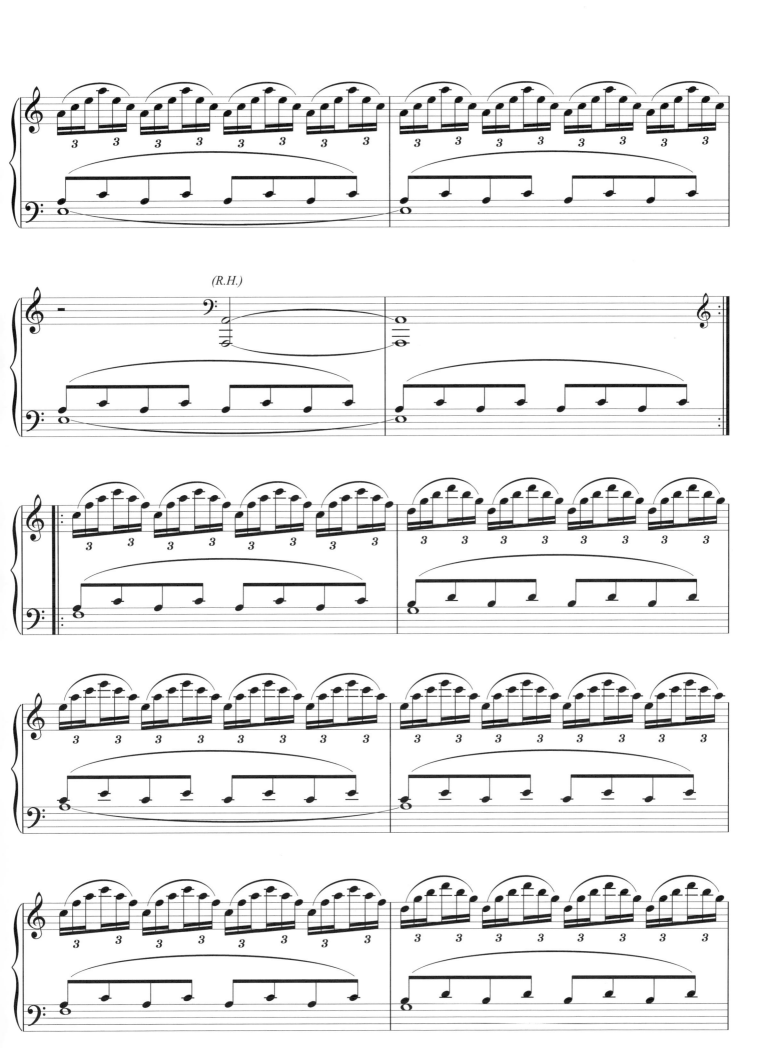

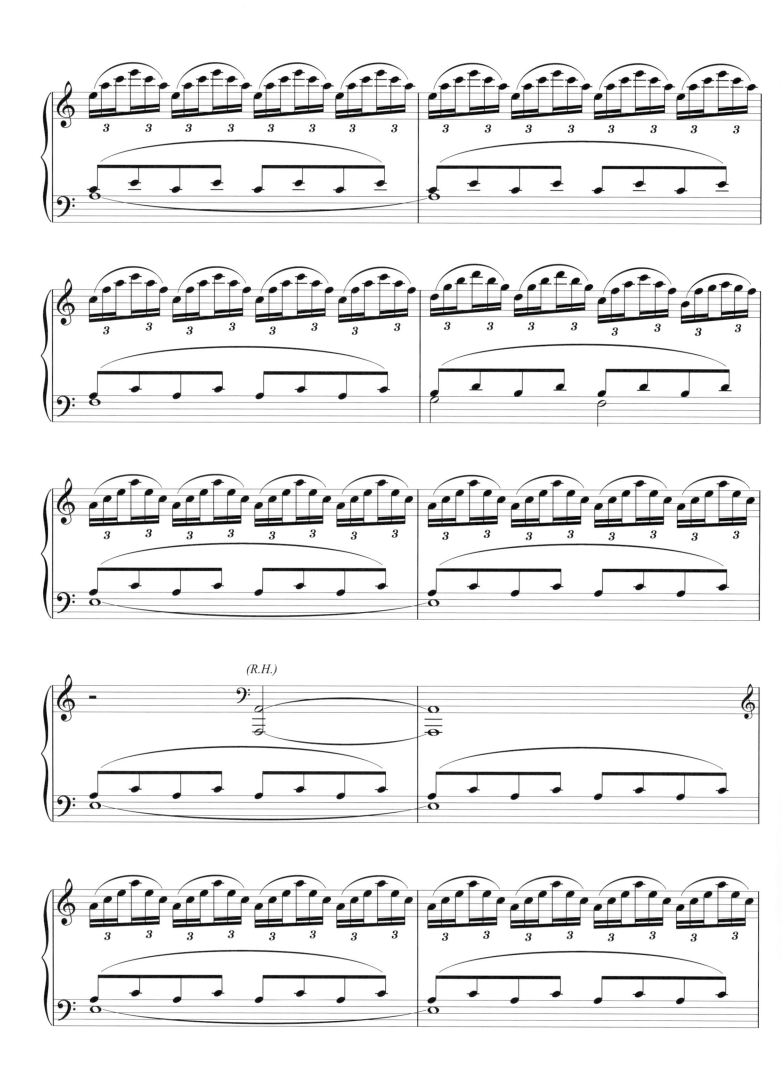

(R.H.)

44

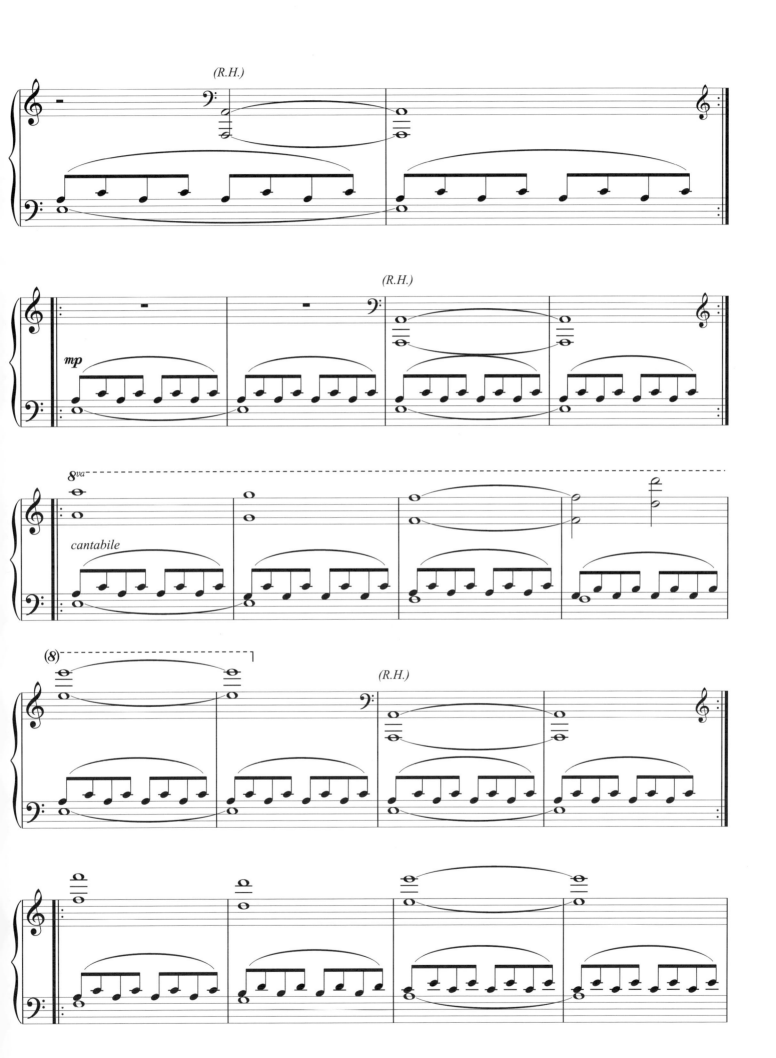

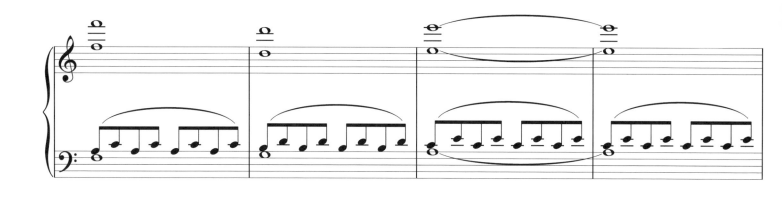

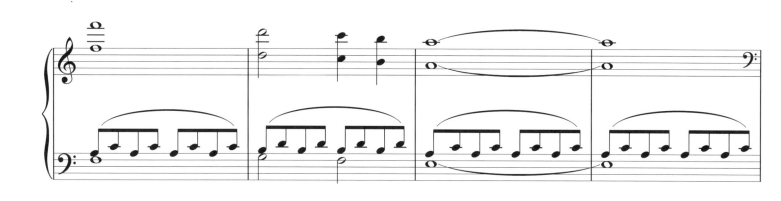

1.

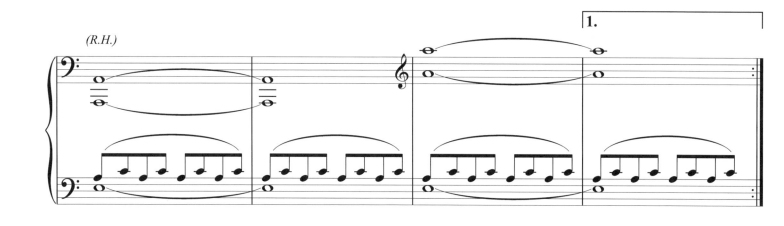

2.

poco rit.

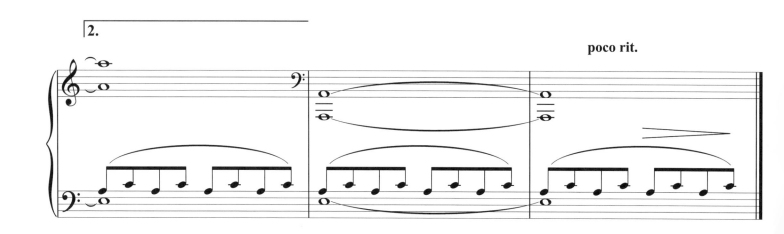

OPUS 38

Music by Dustin O'Halloran.

NOVELETTE IN C MAJOR, I

Music by Francis Poulenc.

Modéré sans lenteur ♪ = 160

56

NUVOLE BIANCHE

Music by Ludovico Einaudi.

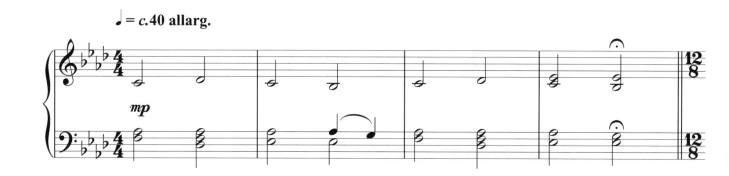

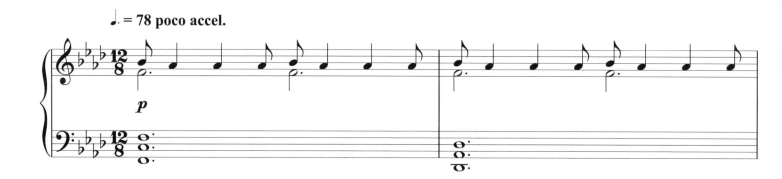

rit.   a tempo

poco a poco accel.

cresc.

60

JULY

(FROM ONCE AROUND THE SUN)

Music by Joby Talbot.

ONE MAN'S DREAM

Music by John Christopher.

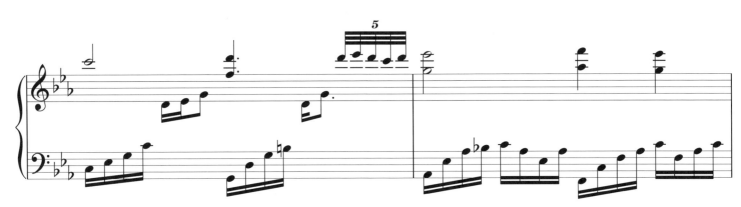

73

ROSEMARY'S WALTZ

(FROM TENDER IS THE NIGHT)

Music by Richard Rodney Bennett.

TOWARDS THE LIGHT

Music by Patrick Hawes.

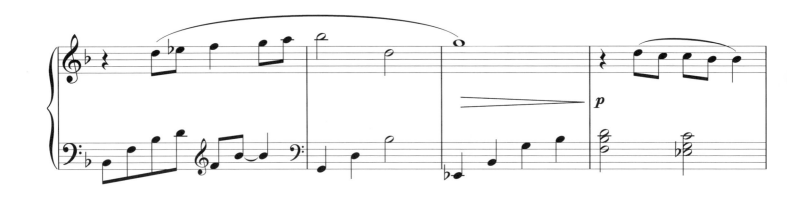

VALSE ROMANTIQUE

Music by Claude Debussy.

VALSE TRISTE

Music by George Fenton.

PRELUDE NO. 5

(FROM SIX PRELUDES)

Music by Lennox Berkeley.

WRITTEN ON THE SKY

Music by Max Richter.

WITH MALICE TOWARD NONE

(FROM LINCOLN)

Music by John Williams.

23456789

Published by
WISE PUBLICATIONS
14-15 Berners Street, London W1T 3LJ,
United Kingdom.

Exclusive Distributors:
MUSIC SALES LIMITED
Distribution Centre, Newmarket Road,
Bury St Edmunds, Suffolk IP33 3YB,
United Kingdom.

MUSIC SALES PTY LIMITED
Units 3-4, 17 Willfox Street, Condell Park,
NSW 2200, Australia.

Order No. AM1009921
ISBN 978-1-78305-827-3
This book © Copyright 2014 Wise Publications,
a division of Music Sales Limited.

Edited by Jenni Norey.
Printed in the EU.

YOUR GUARANTEE OF QUALITY:

As publishers, we strive to produce every book
to the highest commercial standards.

This book has been carefully designed to minimise awkward
page turns and to make playing from it a real pleasure.

Particular care has been given to specifying acid-free, neutral-sized paper
made from pulps which have not been elemental chlorine bleached. This pulp is from
farmed sustainable forests and was produced with special regard for the environment.

Throughout, the printing and binding have been planned to ensure a sturdy,
attractive publication which should give years of enjoyment.

If your copy fails to meet our high standards, please inform us
and we will gladly replace it.

www.musicsales.com